PLANT-TASTIC!
SCATTER!

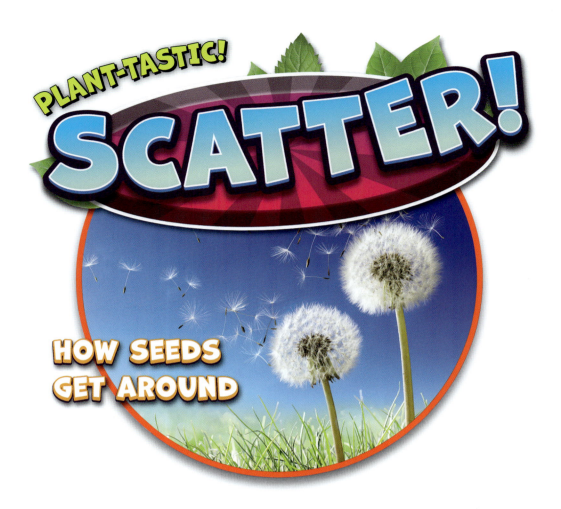

HOW SEEDS GET AROUND

BY REX RUBY

Minneapolis, Minnesota

Credits
Cover and title page, © RomoloTavani/iStock; 4–5, © suefeldberg/iStock; 5, © McKinneMike/iStock; 6, © r.classen/Shutterstock; 7, © James McLauchlan/Shutterstock; 8–9, © wichan yodsawai/iStock; 9, © Aoosthuizen/iStock; 10–11, © Mircea Costina/Shutterstock; 12–13, © Christian Buch/Adobe Stock; 13, © A Daily Odyssey/Shutterstock; 14–15, © BrianAJackson/iStock; 15, © DanielPrudek/iStock; 16–17, © tomas del amo/Shutterstock; 18, © Olenaduygu/Shutterstock; 18–19, © Nahhana/Shutterstock; 20–21, © Maggie/Adobe Stock; 22A, © Konoplytska/iStock; 22B, © Eduardo Vieira DP/Shutterstock; 22C, © mrivserg/Adobe Stock; 22D, © blickwinkel/A. Jagel/Alamy; and 23, © homeworlds/Adobe Stock.

Bearport Publishing Company Product Development Team
President: Jen Jenson; Director of Product Development: Spencer Brinker; Managing Editor: Allison Juda; Associate Editor: Naomi Reich; Senior Designer: Colin O'Dea; Associate Designer: Elena Klinkner; Associate Designer: Kayla Eggert; Product Development Specialist: Anita Stasson

Library of Congress Cataloging-in-Publication Data

Names: Ruby, Rex, author.
Title: Scatter! : how seeds get around / by Rex Ruby.
Description: Minneapolis, Minnesota : Bearport Publishing Company, [2024] | Series: Plant-tastic! | Includes bibliographical references and index.
Identifiers: LCCN 2022058258 (print) | LCCN 2022058259 (ebook) | ISBN 9798888220443 (hardcover) | ISBN 9798888222379 (paperback) | ISBN 9798888223598 (ebook)
Subjects: LCSH: Seeds--Dispersal--Juvenile literature.
Classification: LCC QK929 .R83 2024 (print) | LCC QK929 (ebook) | DDC 581.4/67--dc23/eng/20221215
LC record available at https://lccn.loc.gov/2022058258
LC ebook record available at https://lccn.loc.gov/2022058259

Copyright © 2024 Bearport Publishing Company. All rights reserved. No part of this publication may be reproduced in whole or in part, stored in any retrieval system, or transmitted in any form or by any means, electronic, mechanical, photocopying, recording, or otherwise, without written permission from the publisher.

For more information, write to Bearport Publishing, 5357 Penn Avenue South, Minneapolis, MN 55419.

CONTENTS

A Fruity Meal 4
Cardinal Poop 6
Why Do Seeds Need to Move? 8
Animals Plant Seeds! 10
Hitching a Ride 12
Blowing in the Wind 14
Seeds Sail Away 16
High-Speed Seeds 18
Seeds on the Move 20

Science Lab 22
Glossary 23
Index 24
Read More 24
Learn More Online 24
About the Author 24

A FRUITY MEAL

A hungry cardinal is eating berries from a holly bush. It swallows little berry seeds with each bite of fruit. After its tasty meal, the cardinal flies off to look for more food. The bird doesn't know it, but it has an important job to do. Soon, it will help the holly bush make new plants!

Each holly berry contains four seeds that could become new plants.

CARDINAL POOP

As the cardinal flies through the forest, a blob of its poop falls to the ground. *Splat!* Inside the bird's droppings are seeds from the holly berries it ate. The cardinal has helped scatter the plant's seeds far and wide. Animal poop is just one way seeds get around!

Flowering plants grow their seeds inside fruits that help protect the seeds.

A young holly bush

WHY DO SEEDS NEED TO MOVE?

Many plants can't begin to grow if they are too close to their parent plant. The bigger plants can block sunlight from small **seedlings**. And the nearby soil may not have enough water and **nutrients** for both. If they can't move on their own, the plants need something else to help carry their seeds away.

African elephants eat fruit from marula trees. Then, they poop out the seeds many miles away.

ANIMALS PLANT SEEDS!

Animals can move seeds in other ways, besides in their droppings. Squirrels collect acorns—the seeds of oak trees—and bury them in the ground to save for later. During the winter, squirrels dig up and eat some of the seeds. Any acorns left buried can grow into new oak trees.

Some ants also collect and store seeds underground. The seeds they don't eat grow into new plants, too.

HITCHING A RIDE

Some seeds move around by sticking to animals. Burdock seeds grow together in balls called **burrs**. Each seed is covered in tiny, hooked **spikes**. When an animal brushes past a burdock plant, the burrs stick to the animal's fur. Then, the seeds hitch a ride to a new place!

The spikes on burrs are bent so they can catch onto passing animals.

BLOWING IN THE WIND

A nice **breeze** is all some seeds need to get moving. Maple tree seeds have leafy wings that catch the air. Dandelion seeds are at the ends of fluffy **parachutes** that help them glide along. When the wind blows, these kinds of seeds float up and away.

A poppy plant's seeds are inside a **seedpod** that has tiny holes. When the wind blows, the seeds scatter through the holes.

SEEDS SAIL AWAY

Some seeds float in water to new homes. A coconut palm tree grows large fruit called coconuts. Inside each fruit is a seed. These trees often grow on ocean beaches. When their fruits fall, the fruits and the seeds inside float out to sea. The seeds are carried to beaches miles away.

A coconut's seed is covered by a hard, hairy shell. Around that is a tough outer skin.

HIGH-SPEED SEEDS

Some plants can scatter their seeds by shooting them at high speeds! **Squirting** cucumber plants have hairy, green fruits. Each fruit gets fatter as it grows. It fills with seeds and juice. Finally, the over-full fruit explodes, blasting seeds far from the parent plant. These seeds can travel up to 60 miles per hour (95 kph)!

Unlike the cucumbers people eat, squirting cucumber plants are **poisonous**.

SEEDS ON THE MOVE

Plants have lots of ways to help their seeds move to new places. Some seeds fly in the wind, and others float away in water. Animals help move seeds on their fur and in their poop. With a little help, plant seeds are scattered near and far!

People can also help plants spread to new places by planting seeds!

SCIENCE LAB
BE A SEED DETECTIVE

How do you think the seeds of the plants in these pictures might move to new places?

A

B

C

D

Answers: Seeds in A are eaten and pooped out by animals. The seeds in B float away in the water and C in the wind. The seeds in D stick to passing animals.

GLOSSARY

breeze a light wind

burrs prickly balls of seeds that stick to fur or clothing

nutrients substances that plants need to grow and be healthy

parachutes devices that help things slow down as they fall

poisonous able to kill or harm a person or other animal if eaten

seedlings new, young plants

seedpod a protective case that holds some plants' seeds

spikes hard, sharp points

squirting shooting in a thin stream

INDEX

acorns 10
burrs 12
dandelions 14
elephants 9
fruits 4, 6, 9, 16, 18–19
holly berries 4, 6
maple trees 14
nutrients 8
poop 6, 9, 20, 22
seedlings 8
seedpod 14
squirting cucumber 18–19
water 8, 16, 20, 22
wind 14, 20, 22

READ MORE

Huddleston, Emma. *Seed Dispersers: Poop, Fur, and Other Ways Animals Scatter Seeds (Team Earth)*. Minneapolis: Abdo Publishing, 2020.

Levy, Janey. *How Plants Spread Seeds (The Top Secret Life of Plants)*. New York: Gareth Stevens Publishing, 2020.

Wood, John. *Seeds (Forest School: Outdoor Adventures and Outdoor Play)*. Minneapolis: Bearport Publishing Company, 2022.

LEARN MORE ONLINE

1. Go to **www.factsurfer.com** or scan the QR code below.
2. Enter "**Scatter**" into the search box.
3. Click on the cover of this book to see a list of websites.

ABOUT THE AUTHOR

Rex Ruby lives with his family in Minnesota. He has helped scatter many seeds to new homes.